Recovering Intentional Worship

Some Things To Consider Including in your Church Service

Expanded Edition

David de Bruyn

Recovering Intentional Worship: Some Things to Consider Including in Your Church Service

Published by Religious Affections Ministries
www.religiousaffections.org

Printed in the Unites States of America

ISBN-13 978-0-9824582-1-1
ISBN-10 0-9824582-1-5

Table of Contents

Introduction

When your car has broken down for the umpteenth time, you ask yourself the question: do I fix it or replace it? That kind of choice confronts us with kitchen appliances that break, computer gadgets that fail, and never-ending household repairs. Is it better (and cheaper) to fix what we have or to replace it altogether?

In some ways, that's the choice which confronts the pastor or spiritual leader when he looks at the worship of the church. The worship of the evangelical church has been ravaged by the triviality and banality of popular culture, the unanswerable appeal of pragmatism, and the ubiquitous presence of entertainment. The pastor who cares about offering God the worship He deserves faces the same question: Is it too broken to fix? Do I start over? Do I steadily repair what is broken?

More than likely, every pastor knows the answer. Much as one might wish for it, no one can start from scratch or introduce pristine, biblical worship out of thin air. We must begin with what we have. We are called to particular local churches, with their particular blend of traditions, expectations and understandings of worship. It is not some ideal church with ideal saints that we shepherd, but real people with very real, and often very incorrect, views of worship.

The pastor goes to work in the church to which he is called, looking to God for wisdom for what changes need to be made and at what pace that change must come. Like a craftsman, he hammers here a little and there a little. He judges what must be amputated and what must shrivel by itself. He judges what must be brought back in a hurry and what must be gently cultivated. In some churches the situation is so bad that his repairs will be a near-replacement. In others, he will have to steadily chip and plaster. All along, he seeks to persuade, explaining the reasons for biblical worship, pointing to the beauty of biblical worship, and urging submission to biblical worship. As he does this with meekness and patience, he trusts in God to grant acknowledgment of the truth in his hearers.

In this booklet, I hope to highlight the benefits

of certain worship practices that are sometimes missing from the free-worship traditions. I do not mean to patronize those already doing so; I hope to show how a wise use of these practices can only improve the worship we offer God.

My goal is simply to provoke the thinking of pastors and leaders regarding some of these oft-neglected worship practices. I hope it might encourage those approved and diligent workmen to continue their steady, patient, and rewarding work of shepherding God's flock to worship God appropriately.

Call to Worship

A Call to Worship is often missing from the free worship tradition. Instead, worship in many such churches begins with a warm and friendly welcome, a comment or two about a sports game, the weather, and how happy and blessed the church is that everybody graced the church with their presence. From this chatty start, one is usually directed to a rousing "opening hymn"—an anthem intended to spiritually caffeinate the still-yawning parishioners.

A Call to Worship is not a prescribed element of worship; it is one of the applications of a prescribed element of worship. The prescribed element of worship is the reading of Scripture (1 Timothy 4:13). A Call to Worship is a useful and wise use of the reading of Scripture to prepare the congregation for worship. There is nothing wrong with a warm greeting or welcome and even a preliminary announcement or two. However, beginning corporate worship with Call to Worship achieves many things in one.

First, it calls believers' attention to their purpose in coming. Certainly, as David Peterson argues in *Engaging With God,* believers worship in all of life.[1] However, I'm not convinced that every time we meet the primary task is edification. There are many times when we meet for edification, instruction, fellowship, and service of one another. However, I do think there are times when believers meet for the explicit purpose of hearing and responding to God's Revelation in worship. This is why we are called a spiritual temple (1 Peter 2:5), and changing (or extending) the image, priests offering up praises to God (2:9). This is why Luke says that the church was worshipping in Acts 13:2. The point is, at these times it is necessary to make it known that believers are together in such a meeting to worship. Edification, fellowship, and instruction will all be part of that time, but worship is the primary reason for meeting.

Second, it sanctifies the time. The Call to Worship is like cordoning off a section of time. In doing it, we announce, "What happens here is no

---

1 David Peterson, *Engaging With God* (Downers Grove, IL: InterVarsity Press, 1992), 19.

longer ordinary. Do not profane this time by treating it as ordinary or common. This time is specially set apart for knowing and magnifying God. Stop your normal way of thinking and acting and turn your entire attention to God."

Third, it arrests attention. The Call to Worship is analogous to the blowing of the shofar. At the blowing of the shofar, an assembly was being called, or an announcement was being made. When the words of Scripture call for worship, they simultaneously call for a halt to other activities (including chatting, sipping coffee, and texting). This stands in stark contrast to chatty transitions which are aimed at slowly "warming up" disinterested believers. The Call to Worship breaks into the distracted state of how most enter a church service and demands attention.

Fourth, it demands a response. The Call to Worship is, in fact, a call. God has worship that is due to Him (Ps 29:1-2); the call to worship calls us all to joyfully pay our dues.

The Call to Worship could take more than one form. It could be a simple reading of a portion of Scripture that calls for worship, such as Psalm 95:1-2, 96:1-3, or 100:1-4. It could be a text that celebrates the privilege and joy of worship, such as

Psalm 84 or Psalm 122. It could be a responsive reading between leader and congregation, such as Psalm 118:1-4 or any other appropriate Scripture. A musical Call to Worship could involve the singing of a Scriptural call to worship God by choir or congregation. Because choir "numbers" are often evaluated as performances, I would take special care to direct the congregation to the words being sung, so that it truly performs its function of calling the congregation to worship.

The key is, worship ought not to feel like a movie with several trailers before it really begins. We don't need to transition people into worship with a chatty commentary. When corporate worship is about to begin, it should begin with the authoritative announcement of Scripture. When that is made, believers are now responsible to enter into the posture of corporate worship.

Singing the Psalms

The singing of psalms has all but disappeared from many congregations, unless you count the "As the Deer" chorus as a singing of a psalm. (Lifting the first line from a psalm and adding words about your desire to eventually worship generally doesn't count.) One cannot help feeling that many congregations treat their hymnal as if it is the New Testament and the psalter as if it is the Old: nice, but not really for us.

Psalms by themselves are not adequate for all that New Testament worship aims to be. That is, much as I respect people who want a strict application of the Regulative Principle, I don't think exclusive psalmody is the way to go. Being Old Testament revelation, psalms do not contain all the Christological themes that we want to consider as New Testament believers. However, mixed in with "hymns and spiritual songs"(Eph 5:19, Col 3:16), they are an important part of the worship we ought to offer God.

Why should we return to including psalms in our worship?

1. The psalms were meant to be sung. They are certainly to be studied and taught as the rest of Scripture, but psalms perhaps do not have their fullest effect until clothed again in melody. The psalms are songs, and songs which God's people should sing.
2. Psalms represent the universal experiences of the redeemed. Who has not read a psalm and found David or Asaph's heart-cries resonating with his own? The psalms are experts in experiential theology, experiences of the redeemed shared across dispensations and ages.
3. The psalms are inspired poetry. If we want to view unseen realities properly, there is nothing better than poetry that is inspired by God. The images chosen by God are specifically selected to shape the believing imagination.
4. Psalms cover a variety of themes, from celebration, to confession, to expectation, to cries for deliverance, to wisdom. Therefore, psalms can function as calls to worship,

> confession before the Lord's Supper, preparation before the preached Word, hymns of adoration or thanksgiving, hymns of promise, or even benedictions.

To this, one might add Doug Wilson's plea for psalm singing as one of the means for reversing the feminization of worship that has occurred in the last century. He says,

> The fact that the church has largely abandoned the singing of psalms means that the church has abandoned a songbook that is thoroughly masculine in its lyrics. The writer of most of the psalms was a warrior, and he knew how to fight the Lord's enemies in song. With regard to the music of our psalms and hymns, we must return to a world of vigorous singing, vibrant anthems, more songs where the tenor carries the melody, open fifths, and glory. Our problem is not that such songs do not exist; our problem is that we have forgotten them. And in forgetting them, we are forgetting our boys. Men need to model such singing for their sons.[2]

---

2 Doug Wilson, *Future Men* (Moscow, ID: Canon Press, 2001), 100.

Of course, no one sings a psalm precisely as originally given. Psalms are first translated from Hebrew to our mother tongue, and from there a metrical, rhyming, and often abridged version is made. Nevertheless, we are still singing the substance of the psalms.

Where to find them? There is certainly a revival of psalm-singing in some sectors. Some are re-working the psalms into contemporary metrical tunes. Occasionally, one finds a section of a psalm that has been put to a pleasant and helpful melody, making it something of a cross between a psalm and a spiritual song. Some hymnals include most of the psalms. *The Book of Psalms for Singing,* (Crown & Covenant, 1998), has all of the psalms, many of them set to hymn tunes with which a hymn-singing congregation would be familiar.

Silence

Our fathers had much to say about stillness, and by stillness they meant the absence of motion or the absence of noise or both.

They felt that they must be still for at least a part of the day, or that day would be wasted. God can be known in the tumult of the world if His providence has for the time placed us there, but He is known best in the silence. So they held, and so the sacred Scriptures declare.

—A.W. Tozer, *God Tells the Man Who Cares*

The Scriptures insist on the value of silence in worship, but we seem to fear it. A worship service that is nothing more than an unbroken chain of vocalizations seems like an assault on the ears, to say nothing of the worshipping heart. True worship requires some silence to think, confess, respond, admire. Having a human windmill behind the pulpit giving us a play-by-play of every moment in the service is distracting, to say the least.

We might face an opposite error, in our effort to restore some contemplativeness to worship. We might introduce silence in an arbitrary fashion. Silence in the wrong place is not quietening; it is merely awkward. Instead of using the silence to contemplate, we might merely contemplate the silence and become even more aware of small noises. Instead of directing the gaze of the soul to God, we might become intensely aware of ourselves so that we do not break the silence.

Silence should be natural. Sometimes it might be in slightly longer pauses between elements. Instead of rushing to fill every possible gap with a breezy, chirpy commentary, we might allow a few moments after a song has been sung before moving on. Sometimes it might be during a public prayer, in which the speaker addresses God with natural pauses for thought and admiration, instead of a strange, unpunctuated monologue found nowhere else on earth. Sometimes it might be allowing the congregation's restlessness to fade before beginning the call to worship or the reading of Scripture. Sometimes, it might be a minute's silence after a sermon, to read over the text, pray and make applications, commitments and confessions where necessary. Perhaps it might be in a moment's silent prayer before or after the service.

However it is done, we need to give worshipping hearts time to worship, and give restless hearts time to squirm their way into disciplined silence. From there, perhaps they too will worship.

Stand-alone Scripture Readings

I can't imagine that readers of this book attend churches where the Scriptures are never read during corporate worship. However, we may find that many attend churches where the reading of Scripture is not practiced as an end in itself.

In many churches, the Scriptures are read simply before the sermon or to preface the sermon, as it were. The Scripture reading becomes merely a bridge between the singing and the preaching. I grew up in a setting where a separate, stand-alone reading of Scripture was never practiced. However, I've come to see the tremendous value of this practice for several reasons.

First, it's commanded by precept and example. Paul commanded it in 1 Timothy 4:13 and in Colossians 4:16 and 1 Thessalonians 5:27. It seems John expected the public reading of Scripture too, judging by Revelation 1:3. Early church practice confirms this.

Second, in giving a specific time to the reading of the Word, we testify to our belief in its inspired nature and power to convert. The Word is not merely a tool for our use. The Word itself preaches when it is read. The Word has intrinsic power. (One member of my church was converted simply by reading the book of Matthew.)

Third, we revere God's revelation in our midst when the only sound heard is the Word of God being publicly read. When the Scriptures are read, we call attention to the God-centeredness of Christian worship. Christian worship is entirely a response to what God has revealed about Himself. In the act of stand-alone Scripture readings, we become slow to speak, and quick to listen, so that our worship is a matter of appropriate response, not creative innovation. I have heard this only anecdotally, but it is said that at a certain point during corporate worship in certain Puritan churches, a large pulpit Bible would be marched through the center of the church building and held aloft, while the members all stood in reverence. This is not bibliolatry; this is revering the fact that God has spoken.

Scripture readings might include the text to be preached on for that day, particularly if it is a longer portion. If not, it is a good practice to include more than one reading, perhaps from both Testaments, that deal with a theme similar to that of the text to be preached.

Of late, some helpful tools have emerged, encouraging a careful and skillful approach to the public reading of Scripture. The person who reads Scripture should ideally be one who is skilled at reading and speaking and is able to communicate the text with the inflections and emphases appropriate for the genre of literature and for the subject being addressed. No one is pleased with a flawless but colorless reading of Scripture. Likewise, we want a fluency and freedom in reading that directs our attention to what is being said without tripping over how it is said. This might be natural to some; it is a skill that can be learned and improved in most.

Reiterations and Explanations of Hymns

In 1880 J.S. Curwen wrote *Studies in Worship Music,* an attempt to study the psalms and hymns sung throughout English churches of the time. The final third of the book records Curwen's eye-witness accounts of the churches he visited. The following are some excerpts from his visit to the Metropolitan Tabernacle.

> Mr. Spurgeon evidently takes delight in the service of song, and is anxious above all things that every man, woman, and child in the place should sing. In announcing the hymn he generally makes some remark, such as, "Let us sing joyfully the 48th Psalm,"—"Dear friends, this hymn is full of joy, let's sing it with all our hearts." Occasionally he will stop the congregation, and make them sing more softly

or more quickly, when the effect is at once felt in a surprising degree.

The first hymn on Sunday morning last was "God is our refuge and our strength," to the tune "Evan." Mr. Spurgeon read it slowly through, then he announced the tune and read the first verse again. As the people stood up the precentor advanced from the back of the platform, and started the melody with a clear voice . . . The second hymn was "Thou hidden love of God," to one of the old tunes, "New Creation," made up from Haydn's chorus, "The heavens are telling." This the people enjoyed, and sang as generally as before. The third hymn was "Beneath Thy cross I lay me down," to the tune "Buckingham," which, of course, was a congenial melody. The people were warming to their work, and the volume of sound poured forth more solid and powerful than before. But why should the hymns be read twice through? It may help some illiterate people to understand the words, and Mr. Spurgeon's energetic reading may infuse the devotional spirit of the poet among the congregation; but nearly all the hymns are so well known that these considerations must be of little practical worth. The reading takes up time, and is evidently wearisome to many; besides, it takes away the freshness of the thoughts that are to be uttered.[3]

Some observations are in order. As wearisome at it seemed to Curwen, and as familiar as the hymns were to most, Spurgeon apparently thought it needful to read through each hymn, and make remarks before singing them. Apparently, Spurgeon thought the risk of seeming tedious was worth the benefits brought by such a practice. What could such benefits have been? Here we speculate, using our own experience as a possible guide.

Reading all or certain stanzas of a hymn before singing prepares the mind to work with the heart. The nature of a good melody is to evoke certain affections in us. These we often feel apart from the lyrics. The more challenging the lyrics, the more we find ourselves swooping in and out of conscious comprehension of what we are singing. For a real synergy between head and heart, it is often worthwhile to give the mind a walk-through

---

3 J. Spencer Curwen, *Studies in Worship Music* (London: J. Curwen & Sons, 1880), 429.

of what it will be saying, praying or confessing in song.

Reading the stanzas can stave off musical autopilot. Familiarity tends to lead us to a kind of automatic response. Not all such memorized responses are "vain repetitions," nor do they need to seem new every time we sing them. However, there is something to be said for our love for God being unfeigned—that is, sincere in every way. Words sung with little conscious attention on their meaning can hardly be thought of as fully sincere.

Reading the stanzas of a hymn gives appreciation for what is about to be offered to the Lord. To sing a thing of beauty to the Lord is fitting; to be aware that it is beautiful magnifies the enjoyment of the offering. To find poetic expressions of love for God that take us beyond our own expressions of piety serve to grow and stretch our conceptions of God. However, if these are done while trying to learn or keep up with a melody, the result may be less illuminating than if the mind had been given a few moments to meditate.

Curwen's comments remind us that this can be overdone. Done too often or too frequently, it becomes obnoxious and patronizing. The aim is not to explain what is self-evident or to dissect word-pictures as if they were butterfly abdomen on an entomologist's table. We do not have to explain every "thee" in the hymn or ask repeatedly, "Do we really mean what we're singing?" In my experience, this kind of thing tends to get in the way of worship, rather than assisting it.

However, for many Christians, hymnody may be some of the only serious poetry they encounter. The better the hymnody, typically the greater the comprehension and apprehension gap will be present. If we're going to resist the dumbing down trend, we had better do our share of "lifting up," where appropriate, explanations, reiterations and exhortations.

Planned Prayers

In the free worship tradition, almost nothing is as frowned upon as the idea of prayers that are read or planned. These are seen as the embodiment of vain repetitions and a clear sign of dead formalism and mindless liturgicalism. For years, I thought that unrehearsed, spontaneous, off-the-cuff prayers demonstrated how very real our connection with God was. We spoke with Him as we would anyone else in the assembly. The thought of planning a prayer seemed to me to be some form of fakery, like a boy who finds out what the topic of his impromptu speech is to be and prepares beforehand.

For all my pride in our spontaneity, Tozer's words did seem to represent my experience.

> We of the nonliturgical churches tend to look with some disdain upon those churches that follow a carefully prescribed form of service, and certainly there must be a good deal in such

services that has little or no meaning for the average participant—this not because it is carefully prescribed but because the average participant is what he is. But I have observed that our familiar impromptu service, planned by the leader twenty minutes before, often tends to follow a ragged and tired order almost as standardized as the Mass. The liturgical service is at least beautiful; ours is often ugly.[4]

Tozer's words resonated with me, partly because of how empty most public prayers that I heard were. The typical recipe was: a few stock phrases, some effusive words of praise, the Lord's name repeated like a verbal hiccup, plenty of "we just wanna" and "I pray that," and finished off with the mumbled evangelical incantation, "injeeznameamen." No wonder then that minds wander during prayer when there is little to interest or grip the hearers.

When I first heard public prayers with some thought and planning involved, I was tremendously challenged. My impiety in prayer was exposed to my own heart. My slovenliness in

---

4 A.W. Tozer, *God Tells the Man Who Cares* (Camp Hill, PA: Christian Publications, 1994), 5.

addressing God during public worship was revealed. I was gripped by the importance of leaders modeling right responses to God in their prayers. I began to see that preparing to pray might be a serous task. R. Kent Hughes got my attention when he wrote, "Next to preaching, I spend most of my preparation time on prayer."[5]

At the same time, I seldom lean towards reading a prayer. Spontaneity in prayer is important, because worship must involve responses to God's revelation, not all of which can (or should be) rehearsed. Reading another man's prayer may work for some, but it can feel like reading another man's sermon—all true, but not part of the man who reads it, and the lifelessness is often apparent to the ones listening. As Horton Davies said, "Free prayers, under the guidance of a devout and beloved minister who knows well both his Bible and his people, have a moving immediacy and relevance that set prayers seldom attain."[6] How do we strike a balance between

---

[5] R. Kent Hughes, "Free Church Worship: The Challenge of Freedom," in *Worship by the Book*, D.A Carson, ed. (Grand Rapids, MI: Zondervan, 2002), 175.

[6] Horton Davies, *Christian Worship* (New York: Abingdon, 1957), 68.

soulless reading and mind-numbing informality?

Several writers have given good advice on the topic. Many of them encourage familiarizing oneself with prayers contained in books like *Valley of Vision, Book of Common Prayer,* and Hughes Oliphant Old's *Leading in Prayer: A Workbook for Ministers*. Unless your conscience is troubled at the idea of listening to recorded prayers, there can be value in listening to the prayers of another, from time to time.

The best "practice" for public prayer is private prayer. Praying intelligently in secret will certainly show up in public. Being full of Scripture and Scriptural prayers is crucial. For an extended pastoral prayer, it can be useful to outline some points for the prayer.

Since corporate prayer is said into the ears of both God and the congregation, we have a responsibility to both worship and teach. That requires some thought and planning.

Benedictions

Finishing worship well is as important as beginning it that way. Just as a call to worship consecrates the time for worship, so a benediction allows the last word to be God's blessing and exhortation to His people to continue worshiping as they depart.

There is biblical precedent for this. Almost all the epistles end with some kind of simple blessing. Moreover, scattered through the writings of the apostles are statements of lavish blessing or abundant grace that comes from God to His people. The New Testament authors are fond of blessing their recipients. This becomes even more significant when we consider that the epistles were typically read publicly to the gathered congregations. The local assemblies would have heard Paul, Peter, John, Jude or the writer of Hebrews wishing and praying God's blessings upon them.

Perhaps our free worship tradition has robbed

us of the joy and power of spoken blessings. Perhaps the excesses of the Word-Faith cult have caused us to shrink back from the whole notion of spoken blessings. The people of God have always imitated their Father in blessing and bestowing verbal blessings upon each other. What could be more appropriate than corporate worship concluding with God's promise of enablement, protection, sanctification, or presence?

A benediction is far more than a final nice word or a last pleasantry. A benediction sends worshipers from that consecrated hour with God's own promises to pardon, protect, and be present. For a pastor or appointed spiritual leader to look his people in the eyes and bless them in God's name with God's Words is a particularly tender and poignant moment in the life of a local church. We ought not to underestimate the heartening and strengthening effect of hearing God's promises of goodness to His people. I have seen in the faces of God's people that no small comfort is derived when the last word from the pulpit is one of blessing.

A benediction is also a kind of charge. It reminds God's people what gracious resources go with them as they leave corporate worship to pursue worship in all of life. They are encouraged, but they are also challenged.

Benedictions can take the form of Scripture that is read after the final prayer. Scriptures that readily lend themselves to this function include Numbers 6:24-26, Romans 15:13, 2 Corinthians 13:14, 1 Thessalonians 5:23-24, 2 Thessalonians 2:16-17, Hebrews 13:20-21, 1 Peter 5:10-11, and Jude 24-25. Sometimes other Scriptural texts may be adapted into a blessing or charge without doing violence to the original meaning.

Musical benedictions can be used in place of, or together with, spoken ones. Examples include hymns such as "May the Mind of Christ My Savior," "Be Thou My Vision," "Now May He Who from the Dead," the well-known "Doxology," or some of the texts such as Numbers 6:24-26 or Jude 24-25 set to appropriate music.

Appropriate benedictions send believers off encouraged, fortified and challenged to be ambassadors for Christ in the coming week. They close Christian worship appropriately on a note of hope.

Music For Its Own Sake: Preludes, Postludes and Offertories

Artworks are valued for what they do but not for any immediate function. Art is far from "useless," even though its distinctive value is realized only when it serves no immediate function, when the viewer or listener gives up any immediate self-centered demands on the work and, instead, gives him- or herself up to the work. – Julian Johnson, *Who Needs Classical Music*[7]

Our culture typically uses music as a means to achieve something else. As Johnson says

[7] Julian Johnson, *Who Needs Classical Music?* (New York, NY: Oxford Press, 2002), 39.

elsewhere in his book, most everyday uses of music function as background to some other activity. That's unfortunate and misleading, since music has the potential to be closest in nature to worship itself: an activity we do, not as a means to some other end, but to enjoy the beauty of the object of our affection.

Churches have mimicked this cultural tendency. Purely instrumental music in corporate worship becomes nothing more than a means to an end: to cue the noisy talkers that church is about to begin, to smooth over the awkwardness of passing the collection plates, to get people to be "worshipful" (whatever that is) before the sermon, or to signal to all that the service is over and chatting may resume.

These are not entirely evil uses of instrumental music in church, but if these are all it is used for, it is a goldsmith's tool being used to hammer in a nail. Music has the power and nuance to shape our affections and desires and awake men to transcendent beauty. If it is used as a mere time-cue, a good wolf-whistle might as well substitute. If it is nothing more than "prepping for the sermon," a minute's silence before or after might be just as effective. If music is simply "setting the mood," then some fragrances and pretty pictures could do the trick. For as long as pastors see music as nothing more than a neutral means to some other end, they will perpetuate the problem of musical relativism. People only begin to consider the meaning of music when they are called to do nothing else except listen to the music for its own sake.

Instrumental music in worship services is to be more than decorative. It is to be *formative*: a shaping encounter with beauty in the setting in which beholding God's beauty is our aim. To consider the shape and form of a beautiful melody, an ingenious arrangement and a skilful performance are not unspiritual ends. They are not some effete aesthetic snobbery far removed from the meat-and-potatoes of preaching the Word – and I say that as a preacher. Instrumental music in corporate worship is taught by Colossians 3:16, and supported by Old Testament example. The Psalms seem to make it clear that beautiful music offered in worship, glorifies God. "Sing unto him a new song; play skilfully with a loud noise." (Ps 33:3)

Yes, there are risks. In a culture that uses music as entertainment, "wordless" music tends to raise only two questions in the average listener: 1) How does this make me feel? 2) How well was it performed? And in keeping with this, all too many church offertories have become nauseating displays of flamboyant and inappropriate musical acrobatics. Too many instrumentals are just chord-changing games to help the swaying, closed-eyed worshippers with their quest for intense emotion. Hence, the pastor concerned with a vertical focus in worship all too often rushes to fill those times with projected words on a screen, or to dispense with them altogether. In so doing, we cut off a vital part of worship and perpetuate a consumeristic approach to worship's most exquisite tool.

Of course, overcoming a whole cultural tendency is not a task to be sniffed at. Moreover, clumsy attempts to encourage a thoughtful consideration of music may end up distracting worshippers and raising all kinds of objections about the place of art in the church. We had best approach this knowing that most worshippers are expecting nothing more than mood-music and will resist calls to apply their thinking to music itself. And yet, as men concerned with doing more than making church seem familiar, we ought to be obedient to Scriptural example and seize this opportunity to shape the affections of our people.

I suggest that at certain times, attention is specifically drawn to the preludes, postludes, offertories, or other forms of special instrumentals, either by someone leading the service, or on a bulletin or projection. Stating the name of the piece and its composer at the very least draws attention to the music as an object: a work of art made *by* someone *for* someone. If possible, some remarks can be made about the form of the music: the shape of the melody, its harmonies, or a remark which draws attention to the music. This does not have to be done every time (I would say it should not, in fact), nor do the remarks have to be so technical as to invite criticism that they are pretentious. A simple gesture toward the music will suffice, helping people to not simply use the music for a personal mood-change, but to consider the music until its meaning and beauty come home to the worshipper, regardless of mood and feeling at the time. And then, we don't need to be embarrassed about this exercise and show slides of waterfalls and mountains with Psalms quoted at the bottom. Yes, we really can let people do nothing but listen to music for several minutes.

It may be that as a result of these instrumental offerings the worshippers will be better prepared to sing, or pray, or listen to the Word. If so, fine. However, this is not why we ought to include these. We want a Scripturally-prescribed encounter with beauty, skill, order, and glory in the presence of corporate worship.

Doxologies and Gloria Patris

A hymn to complete another hymn, or a hymn to complete a section of worship, is how we might think of singing the *Doxology* and the *Gloria Patri*. The *Doxology* known to most Protestants was composed by Thomas Ken in the 17th century, and a common version of the *Gloria Patri* was composed by Charles Meineke (1782-1850). This is the so-called Lesser Doxology, the Greater Doxology being the *Gloria in Excelsis*, still used in the Catholic Mass.

The idea behind doxologies comes from Scripture itself, where a section of Scripture is concluded with a doxology. Paul does this (Romans 11:36, Galatians 1:5, and Ephesians 3:21), and each of the five books of the Psalms ends with a doxology (Psa 41:13, 72:18-19, 89:52, 106:48, 150:1-6) The tradition of singing doxologies at the end of hymns goes back to the synagogue and ancient Christian worship.

Besides biblical and historical reasons, a church might consider using doxologies for some practical reasons. First, it roots us in a robust Trinitarian worship. Our worship should never be so generically monotheistic that its distinctive Trinitarian emphasis is lost. We worship the God who is Three. We address the Father, through the Son, by the Spirit. We honor Christ, who is the radiance of the Father, of whom the Spirit testifies. We praise the Spirit, who is the Lord, and whose fellowship enables us to know the Father's love for the Son, and the Son's love for the Father.

Second, the doxology promotes a healthy catholicity and sense of the call for universal worship. In singing the *Doxology* we call on creatures here below and the heavenly hosts above to worship with us. As hymns such as "All Hail the Power of Jesus' Name," "Holy God We Praise Thy Name," and "All Creatures of Our God and King" do, the *Doxology* calls on more than simply our local congregation to praise God. It echoes Psalm 150- everything that breathes has an obligation to worship.

In some ways, these are extended "Amens." and used well, unite a congregation in its commitment to the historic faith and the obligation for all to worship the Triune God of that faith.

Hymn Choices

When we select the songs and hymns for corporate worship, there are plenty of weak, cowardly, and even evil reasons to motivate our choices: sheer familiarity, a pledge of allegiance to a certain tribe within Christianity, a desire to attract or placate certain constituencies in the church, or the desire to appear moderate, balanced, and relevant in the eyes of man. Since what we sing is an offering to the Lord, our selection should be guided by the question, is this hymn *good*? *Good*, not in the sense that it brings me pleasure, but *good* in that it does well what it was meant to do. It is well-crafted, excellent, beautiful, and useful for worship. Whether or not I like what is good does not change what is good, it is simply a commentary on me. If I do not like what is good, I have a biblical responsibility to learn what it is and to come to love it (Phil 1:9-11). How do we determine if a hymn or song is good? I suggest a start might be these five questions.

1) Is it truthful (Phil 4:8)? Truth is what corresponds to reality. Music and poetry are creations of God and can depict reality as God has made it, or falsify it. The lyrics of the songs sung must be doctrinally correct and orthodox, while allowing for poetic license. Hymns are not doctrinal statements put to music, nor should they be. They are poems, using metaphor, rhyme and meter. These poems, given their form, must nevertheless communicate Scriptural truth.

While music does not communicate propositions, it communicates sentiments, emotions and affections. In this way, the music can falsify what is being sung in different ways. It can communicate a mood or a sentiment contrary or unlike what the text purports to speak of, e.g. galloping when speaking of "sinking deep in sin" or waltzing at the thought of Jesus returning, or laughing or revelling at the thought of God's holiness. In such cases, not only is the music inappropriate for the text, it misleads believers into associating those emotional states with the truths being sung.

Music can also trivialize a profound truth, exaggerate an emotion, distract from the subject matter, and encourage a narcissism when singing.

All these responses are possible due the actual form of the music. The form chosen must communicate affective truth, inasmuch as the lyrics must communicate propositional truth.

2) Does it evoke ordinate affection (Mal 1:11)? God is a unique Being, and there is a kind of love that corresponds to knowing His being and a kind that does not. The music and the poetry should, through the meaning of their form, evoke *appropriate* joy, fear, contrition, thanksgiving, and delight. Church leaders must discern between kinds of joy, or kinds of fear, and know when particular music evokes those affections.

When hymns and songs sung are merely exercises in self-gratification or entertainment, the emphasis is no longer one of responding to the Being of God. They are merely vehicles for self-love, and when offered to God,that makes them acts of profanity or even idolatry.

Ordinate affection arises from the commitment to know God as He is, to submit to Him entirely, to grant Him appropriate responses, be they foreign or uncomfortable to us. This is the fear of the Lord, which is the beginning of wisdom.

3) Is it a worthy offering (Psalm 33:1-3)? Worship music is not primarily offered to man for his enjoyment, though he is invited to worship the Lord with gladness. The One who hears all and understands all music and poetry deserves our most skilful and excellent musical and poetic offerings. This means selecting the best hymns that are beautiful and most expressive of God's manifold glories. Though cost, skill-level, and spiritual maturity may limit or hinder the quality of what is offered, we should always aim to do the best with what we have and to keep improving. God accepted the birds which the poor Israelite would offer; He did not accept the bruised offerings which the priests in Malachi's day offered.

4) Can mature believers understand and use it (1 Cor 14:15)? Paul desires that believers sing with understanding. On one level, every human being is capable of perceiving beauty, being made in the image of God. People's levels of appreciation may differ, but no one is deaf or blind to transcendence. When music is true, good, and beautiful, it will speak to all men everywhere. At the same time, our current cultural impoverishment means that many find serious and beautiful music and poetry impenetrable. When the good is no longer familiar, the church faces the hard task of making it familiar without causing people to choke on what they have no capacity to swallow. The solution is not to give people regular "hits" of pop music and banal lyrics so as to placate their cravings (for this will only feed habits that ought to be left to die), but to expose the church to great works, explain them, and allow people to get used to them through repetition and regular use. Works that are simpler or more familiar (yet still beautiful or helpful), should be mixed with those that are more ornate in their beauty, to give beginners and the immature some "rungs on the ladder" to climb up. As elevation of thought and beauty increases, accessibility must be maintained through regular explanations, regular exposure, and regular use.

5) Does it respect both tradition and contemporaneity? *Traditional* and *contemporary* are regrettably misunderstood and misused terms in the music debate. *Traditional* hymnody ought to mean the music and hymns which belong to the genuine Christian tradition, having equivalent sentiments, regardless of differences in era, doctrinal tradition, or culture. *Contemporary* hymnody ought to refer to music and poetry written by Christians in our era that continues these affections, universal to Christian experience over two millennia, and reports them according to 21st-century experience, in equivalent forms that answer to the 21st-century imagination. Instead, *traditional* is commonly used to mean hymns older than fifty years (including trite, useless hymns from the 19th century), and *contemporary* is used to refer to pop/rock forms of music and their latest derivatives.

Used in these uncritical ways, a church should be neither "traditional" nor "contemporary" in its musical choices, for there is no virtue in simply using older hymns for the sake of their age or using pop/rock as a deferring nod to relevance and contemporaneity.

When the terms are used correctly, Christian leaders should aim for both in corporate worship. The church should honor and enjoy its heritage by knowing, learning, and singing the hymns and songs that belong to the genuine Christian tradition. This should ideally represent a wide spread of eras and even doctrinal traditions, to celebrate the true catholicity of the faith. This both honors our elders and keeps us exposed to the examples of our forbearers' worship. It reveals our own blind-spots, and the excesses and weaknesses of our own era.

At the same time, the contemporary church must use its own voice, and its own words, to worship God, for this is commanded of us. Contemporary hymns and songs and music that represent art good enough to carry the weight of worship ought to be used. Songs written in our era should not be used simply because they are familiar; they should be used because they are genuinely good, whether or not they are familiar to us. If they are genuinely good and yet not familiar, they ought to be used until they become familiar. This applies to the traditional hymns too.

It is a malady of modernism to define ourselves in terms of time, to obsess about progress and novelty, and to regard tradition with suspicion or disdain. Christian who understand the importance of carrying on the faith that has been handed down should oppose this attitude, and one good way is to conserve, create, and transmit good hymnody.

Creeds

"My faith has found a resting place, not in device nor creed." So goes the hymn, and if taken over-literally, we might agree. Our faith does not rest in a creed, or even in propositions that explain the gospel. Our faith rests upon the person and work of Jesus Christ, which the propositions of the gospel are essential to properly explain. This is partly what the ancient creeds do.

The ancient ecumenical creeds served as bulwarks against error and rallying calls to orthodoxy. They demarcated the boundaries of the Christian faith, as defined in response to heresies present in those eras. In the early centuries, the heresies were particularly Christological and Trinitarian ones, which is why the Apostles', Nicene, and Athanasian creeds and Formula of Chalcedon focus on the person and nature of Christ and His relationship to the Father and the Spirit.

What is the use of creeds for those of us in the

free worship tradition? Several come to mind.

First, in an age of doctrinal vacillation and theological innovation, we can all do with regular reminders of some of the fundamentals of the faith. Granted, the creeds do not exhaustively cover every fundamental tenet of Christianity, but then no creed could. Fundamentals are only properly recognized when the gospel comes under threat in some way. We do not know how many ways the gospel may be denied, and in that sense, the fundamentals are not a bounded set. What the ancient creeds achieve are fairly concise statements of several doctrines fundamental to the faith: Trinitarianism, the virgin birth, the deity and humanity of Christ, His crucifixion, resurrection, and return, the reality of future resurrection and judgment, the forgiveness of sins, and the existence of the church. These creeds, given their age, provide us with a fairly impressive sketch of the gospel, unchanged in seventeen centuries. Recited together, they are like a "pledge of allegiance" to the gospel.

Second, in an age of amnesia regarding our Christian heritage, creeds state our solidarity with the saints triumphant. We recognize that the faith once delivered to the saints has been taught to faithful men, who taught others also, until it arrived in our hands. It is not as if the gospel has been in total eclipse until the last two hundred years or so. Creeds promote a "small-c" catholicity: we belong to the universal church – past, present, and future.

Of course, those in the free-church and Baptist traditions have some understandable concerns. Rightly used, creeds cannot be coercive statements which demand assent. They function rather like miniature summaries of Christian belief, by which any gospel-believing Christian could express as a concise statement of his own orthodox beliefs.

Advocates of the Regulative Principle of Worship rightly ask: where are creeds commanded by Scripture by precept or by example for use in worship? Answer: to the degree that creeds function as a form of teaching, they are simply an application, or a circumstance, of the element that is explicitly commanded: the teaching of God's Word. A creed distils and teaches apostolic doctrine. To recite it is to hear instruction, albeit from the third or fourth centuries.

Finally, what of some of those difficult statements: "descended into hell," "baptism for the remission of sins," "holy catholic church"? These take some explaining, but they are hardly insurmountable obstacles. Even those of us who do not hold to baptismal regeneration can explain the baptism for the remission of sins using Acts 2:37. "Catholic" need not refer to the Roman church, but to the universal church. Catholic transliterates the Greek *katholikos,* which simply means universal. Some churches have substituted the word *universal* for *catholic* to deal with its Roman associations. The phrase "descended into hell" is missing from several ancient copies of the creed,[8] but even if we include it, we have Scriptures such as Acts 2:31 and 1 Peter 3:19 to explain this. The question is, is it worth all that explaining?

In my judgment, yes. What is gained in terms of "gospel-literacy," catholicity, and sense of Christian patrimony is worth the effort. Whether they are read and recited together, or whether they are simply studied as a lesson, I heartily commend recovering some use of the ancient creeds in the worship and teaching ministry of the church.

---

8 See Wayne Grudem's discussion of this in his *Systematic Theology* (Nottingham: Intervarsity Press, 1994), 582-594.

Conclusion

Josiah may have been one of the bravest men who ever lived. Receiving the kingdom with the sword of God's impending judgment dangling over its head, Josiah set about reforming the worship of Judah with an almost frenzied diligence. He cleansed and repaired the Temple, destroyed idolatrous shrines, altars, and images, defiled the high places of idol worship (making them unusable), expelled spiritists and mediums, defrocked apostate priests, re-instituted the Passover, and did his best to see a radically monotheistic Israel worship God according to the Law.

Josiah did all this knowing that he would not be able to turn back the clock and undo what his religious forebearers had done. And yet, the epitaph on his life was this: Now before him there was no king like him, who turned to the LORD with all his heart, with all his soul, and with all his might, according to all the Law of Moses; nor after him did any arise like him (2 Kings 23:25).

Pastors and spiritual leaders like Josiah are rare, but they do exist. They labor with the sense of how difficult it will be to restore biblical worship to the church, but they labor nonetheless. They understand that they may not be able to turn back the juggernaut of pragmatism that has overwhelmed the worship of the evangelical church. Nevertheless, they do not throw up their hands in despair or curse the futility of it all. They quietly, gently, but persistently insist upon biblical worship in their churches. They throw out what is useless. They challenge accepted practice if it is not commanded in Scripture. They re-introduce what has been commanded but forgotten. They labor against the momentum of the culture, against the popularity of majority opinions in the worship-wars, and sometimes even against the approval of those in their churches.

Like Josiah, they have to begin somewhere. What they have been handed may not be great, but it is what they have, and they set about the task of fixing, restoring, cleansing, and building. At times, the progress seems like swimming upstream, but they persist.

Though Josiah's reforms were soon swallowed

up by Judah's seemingly unstoppable apostasy, God saw fit to honor his memory with a glowing tribute in the eternal Word of God. The outward success of worship warriors may be unimpressive, but there is One who sees.

If our children and our children's children are able to find churches where biblical worship still exists in their day, it will be because of Josiah-like pastors and leaders who are trying to reform worship in our day. If this booklet has helped them in their labors, then God be praised.

www.ingramcontent.com/pod-product-compliance
Lightning Source LLC
La Vergne TN
LVHW010543100826
845148LV00013B/2584